Comprehension

Book 1

Jonny Zucker

Hopscotch

A division of MA Education Ltd

Published by Hopscotch
A division of MA Education Ltd
St Jude's Church
Dulwich Road
Herne Hill
London SE24 0PB

Tel: 020 7738 5454

© 2008 MA Education Ltd

Written by Jonny Zucker
Series design by Blade Communications
Cover illustration by Susan Hutchison
Illustrated by Fliss Cary

ISBN 978-1-90430-720-4

Acknowledgments
The authors and publisher gratefully acknowledge permission to reproduce copyright material in this book.

'Sounds' by Irene Rawnsley, from *The Works*

'Who is My Neighbour?' By David Harmer

Every effort has been made to trace the owners of copyright of material in this book and the publisher apologises for any inadvertent omissions. Any persons claiming copyright for any material should contact the publisher who will be happy to pay the permission fees agreed between them and who will amend the information in this book on any subsequent reprint.

CONTENTS

Today, more than ever, it is important that children can read and interpret text in many different forms. Traditional narrative is still important but, increasingly, vital information is now presented in a wide range of formats including graphs, flow charts, diagrams, timelines, pictures and illustrations. The overwhelming abundance of information available from internet sources places increasing demands on children to locate, sort, understand and interpret information more quickly than ever before. This series aims to help children develop strategies that will enable them to succeed in our information-overloaded world!

About this series

Comprehension is a series of books aimed at developing key comprehension skills across Key Stage 1, Key Stage 2 and the first years of Key Stage 3.

The series aims to set the children thinking. It requires them not only to interpret what they read but to use the information they have gathered in a constructive way, by applying it to, for example, graphs, maps, diagrams, pictures and tables. Alternatively, many of the activities require the children to explain in words information that is contained in different visual representations, such as graphs, diagrams and illustrations. The **Comprehension** series aims to stimulate children so that they see things from a different perspective and respond in a variety of ways.

There are six books in the series.

> Ages 5-6
> Ages 6-7
> Book 1 – Year 3
> Book 2 – Year 4
> Book 3 – Year 5
> Book 4 – Year 6

Each book aims to:
❑ develop children's inferential skills, encouraging them to 'read between the lines' where they have to search for hidden clues or make a link between cause and effect;
❑ develop children's deductive skills, enabling them to relate information in the text to their own experiences and background knowledge;
❑ develop children's evaluative skills to encourage critical evaluation and expression of opinion;
❑ encourage enjoyment and curiosity as well as develop skills of interpretation and response.

Each book is divided into ten fiction and ten non-fiction activities.

Many of the activities are cross-curricular, taking in aspects of science, history and geography, for example. Other activities are centred around the interests of children, and topics such as magic, Martians, wizards and dragons are included. All the activities are intended to be fun as well as purposeful!

Using the activities

The activities are versatile enough to be used as part of whole-class lessons, group work or homework / reinforcement tasks. The teacher's role is to introduce the activity, carry out any revision of terms that may be necessary and put the task into a suitable context. Many of the activities would benefit from being discussed in pairs or small groups before commencing.

It is important to stress to the children that they read the complete text (including the required tasks) before they actually do anything. This helps to ensure they understand what they have to do before they begin. Their answers could be formulated in note form before reading through the activity again to make sure there has been no misunderstanding.

Name _____

Highway danger

The wind blew silently across the dark field and the clock struck once. There was no one to be seen apart from a shadowy figure wrapped in a black cloak on horseback. He called quietly to the horse and started to gallop across the field and into a dark lane. He had only gone a little way when suddenly from out of the bushes appeared three men on horseback carrying lanterns and holding pistols. They were shouting at him at the tops of their voices. They were highwaymen and they wanted his money. He luckily had his own gun and fired it once in the air. All of the horses neighed with fright and the man began to gallop away from the highwaymen as fast as he could, with them following close behind.

❑ Read the story extract above and then answer the questions below. Write your answers on another sheet of paper.

1. Where is the story set? Did you find it an interesting story setting? Would it make you want to read the rest of the story? Explain why/why not.

2. What do you think are the three most exciting phrases used in this story?

3. Write some words and phrases of your own that describe the scene.

4. Look at the words below that appear in this text. Write some words that could replace them.

shadowy _____

pistols _____

started _____

shouting _____

5. What do you think might happen after this opening scene of the story? List five possible events in the story.

Name _____

Martian meeting

One evening Mr Gothic was on his way home from work when he says he saw a flying spaceship land in a paint factory car park. He told a local newspaper reporter that what he thought must have been a Martian came out of the spacecraft and tried to talk to him.

Here is Mr Gothic's description of what happened. It describes the scene at the start of the story:

I saw him at about 7pm on the way home from work. I had to contact the newspaper – I didn't do it for the money. I only asked for two hundred pounds and they gave me a hundred.

The Martian was definitely green. Green from head to foot. I mean feet. He had four feet and on each foot there were seven toes. He had these two huge heads. One had two eyes and the other one only had one eye. On the head with one eye he was wearing a pink baseball cap that said 'Hockey Team'.

Instead of hands he had these three sort of long flipper things, about twice the size of a human arm. At the end of each one of these flippers were these two stumpy fat fingers, each one with a very long blue nail at the end. His green body was covered in these weird scales, a bit like a fish.

I was really scared after I'd seen him. It must have been about 6.30pm by then and I drove home really quickly to tell my wife about the experience.

1. Why do you think Mr Gothic went to his local paper with the story?

2. From Mr Gothic's description, what do you think are the three key phrases he uses to describe the Martian? Underline them.

3. What in Mr Gothic's description suggests that he was possibly making the whole story up?

4. Draw a picture of the martian as described by Mr Gothic.

Name _____

The derelict building

❑ Look at this picture.

1. Complete this story beginning using the information in the picture.

Sheree crossed at the _____ and then raced along

_____ Lane, past the _____shop. She almost tripped

over the legs of an _____ _____ who was sitting on a bench

outside the _____. She stopped to catch her breath,

leaning against the _____ _____ sign. Then she saw the building.

It was _____ storeys high with a row of _____ chimney pots

on the tall roof. The two top windows were boarded up and the shop

front had a sign saying _____ _____ across it. She could see a door

that was _____. She looked thoughtfully at the stairs on the

_____ and decided to climb up them. Little did she know what a

huge mistake that was going to be!

She pulled open the huge door at the top of the stairs and...

2. Write what you think happens next.

Name _____

Questions and exclamations

❑ Some of these pictures represent questions and some represent exclamations.

A question looks like this: Are you going to the shop after school?

An exclamation looks like this: Give that ball to me!

❑ In each picture write a question or an exclamation in the speech bubble.

❑ On another sheet of paper, write three exclamations about being late for school.

❑ Then write three questions asking what one of your friends will be doing in the school summer holidays.

Name _____

The field find

❑ Read the following passage carefully. All the dialogue is in bold.

The boiling sun beat down on Longton Primary School. It had been like this for two weeks. On this particular day most of the school was sitting in the shade of trees on the school field instead of shouting and running around.

Kate was digging in the field with an old plastic spade she'd found. Her best friend Abbey was watching.

"Waste of time," moaned Abbey.

"Maybe we'll find something valuable," said Kate.

"Don't be silly," replied Abbey, **"there's nothing down there at all, just earth and worms."**

Suddenly Kate held up something gold and shiny.

"Look! Look! It's like the one we saw in that book about the Romans. It's got a face on one side and some funny writing on the other."

Kate started running. Abbey was close behind.

Kate knocked on the staff room door. Mr Thomas answered it. Kate blurted out **"We've found something incredible sir!"** Mr Thomas pulled a face that he only pulled when he knew someone was telling him a strange story. He held the object in his hand and a smile appeared on his face.

"Nice try girls," he laughed, **"but this is a very clever copy of the real thing. I found one in my Super Flakes at breakfast yesterday morning. Try again. You never know, you may have better luck next time!"**

❑ Use the dialogue to answer the questions below. Write your answers on another sheet of paper.

1. Is Abbey as keen as Kate about digging for treasure? How do you know?
2. Why was the school field quieter than normal?
3. Why doesn't Abbey think Kate has a chance of finding buried treasure?
4. What does Kate think she's found?
5. What does Mr Thomas think of their story?
6. How did Mr Thomas know it was a fake?

Name _____

The magician learns

❏ Read about The Great Alfonso and answer the questions. Write your answers on another sheet of paper.

The Great Alfonso wasn't a very good magician. 'Why can't I get the tricks right?' he often thought. Despite this, people were always booking him for children's parties.

"We hear you're hilarious," Mrs Lynch told him when she phoned up to see if he was free for her daughter's birthday.

1. What does The Great Alfonso say to himself?
2. Why do you think Mrs Lynch says The Great Alfonso is 'hilarious'?

The Great Alfonso decided one day to get much better at his tricks. "I am going to make sure I improve," he told his son Albert.

"Yeah yeah, Dad," replied Albert, not looking up from his comic and shrugging his shoulders. "Same old story."

3. Why do you think Albert shrugs his shoulders?

But The Great Alfonso was not one to be put off. He went to a magic shop and bought a set of new tricks and a book that took you through each trick step-by-step. "I'll show them!" he kept on telling himself. He arrived at Mrs Lynch's house on the afternoon of her daughter's birthday.

"Ah the great man himself!" she exclaimed, trying to hide her smile.

4. What phrase does he keep on using to drive himself on?
5. What sort of tone of voice do you think Mrs Lynch uses when The Great Alfonso arrives at her house?

When The Great Alfonso walked into the party room all of the children started cheering and calling out at him. He started with some card tricks and to everyone's surprise they worked. Then he pulled a toy rabbit out of a top hat and made it disappear again. Every trick he did worked perfectly. The children loved the show and he got a huge cheer at the end.

"Well," said Mrs Lynch bringing him a cup of tea, "I really like your new show. I'd heard that you got everything wrong and that your show was funny because of that."

6. What might the children have been calling out at him?
7. What word could replace 'said' to show how Mrs Lynch felt?

Name _____

Sounds

❑ Complete the following poem.

The tiniest sound in the world must be

A little green caterpillar eating his _____.

The spookiest _____ in the world must _____

A ghost singing songs in a hollow _____.

The noisiest sound in the _____ must be

Thunder pushing mountains into the _____.

The _____ sound in the world must be

Our baby chuckling when she _____ with me.

❑ Add another verse of your own to the poem.

❑ Draw pictures to go with each verse.

Name _____

Robot interview

❑ Alfie has invented a robot that does lots of jobs around the house. He's been invited onto Bob Diamond's television show 'Diamond Chat' to be interviewed about his robot. Here's a script of the interview.

Bob: So Alfie, tell us first how you got the idea to make this robot.
Alfie: Well Bob, I was getting a bit tired of tidying my room and doing the washing up.
Bob: How did you start making it?
Alfie: First of all I needed a big old television set for its body.
Bob: And where did you find one of those?
Alfie: Our neighbours bought a flash new TV so they gave me their old one.
Bob: And then what?
Alfie: I needed some shopping trolley wheels to place underneath the TV to make the robot move. My local supermarket were throwing out some broken trolleys, so they gave me six pairs of wheels.
Bob: Fascinating!
Alfie: At each side of the TV is a long piece of metal with a baseball glove at the end. These 'arms' are attached to the TV on a rotating ball. This means the 'arms' can move around. The gloves are what carry out the robot's work.
Bob: What went on top of the TV?
Alfie: I needed a flat screen computer monitor with five light bulbs on top of it. The computer shop donated these because I agreed to paint their name (Mac Superstore) on the front of the TV.
Bob: Wow!
Alfie: Each light bulb has a thin metal wire coming out from its top with a tiny square box at the end. Inside each box is a microchip. These microchips receive commands from my control box.
Bob: Are we going to see your robot?
Alfie: Of course! It's just backstage. I'll go and get it now.

1. How many different things did Alfie need to make his robot? List them.

2. Draw a labelled picture of the robot based on the information given in the interview.

3. Name five household jobs you think the robot might carry out, that were not mentioned in the interview.

Name _____

Skateboard hero

1. Look at the words beside various parts of this scene. Replace each one with a word that creates a greater impact on the reader.

2. Write a paragraph describing this scene. Use as many exciting words as possible.

Name _____

Farmer Giles

Farmer Giles shut the door. It had been a long, hard day in the fields with his sheep. The wind got to him. It spoke in icy tones. He threw another two logs on the fire and sat in his favourite chair.

1. What does 'The wind got to him' mean?
2. What 'spoke' to Farmer Giles?

It had already been a long winter and it was only October. The weather forecast said it was going to improve but Farmer Giles didn't believe this. He'd had a phone call from his sister Mary that afternoon. She lived on another farm about five miles away. She said getting to the shops had nearly been impossible, what with the snowfall on her drive.

3. Does he think the weather is going to improve? What words tell you this?
4. Why had Mary found it so hard to go shopping?

Farmer Giles turned on the radio and listened to his favourite music programme. Within a few minutes he was fast asleep and dreaming about his boyhood days growing up on his dad's farm. He'd started working in the fields with sheep and cows from a very young age. The ringing tones awoke him and he quickly sat up.

5. What woke Farmer Giles?

It was his sister Mary again. She told him the snow had stopped and that she'd be coming to visit him tomorrow. He frowned for a second as he'd wanted to watch the cricket all day. He'd always been a big cricket fan and apart from the news it was the only thing he ever really watched on television. At the end of the conversation he smiled. She was a good sister. Seven years his senior, she'd always looked out for him. He turned the radio up a little louder.

6. Did he want Mary to visit him? How do you know?
7. Is Mary older or younger than him? How do you know?

Name _____

How to look after house plants

House plants need special care if they are to grow well. When buying a house plant, check to see if it is healthy. Do not buy plants that have brown or diseased leaves. Always read the label that comes with the plant. This will tell you how to care for it properly. Place your plant where it can get some sunlight but do not place it too close to a window where it may get too cold at night. Water the plant regularly but do not over water it as this can damage the roots. Feed the plant regularly with special plant food. Repot when necessary.

1. Underline in blue all the things you should do to look after a house plant correctly.

2. Underline in red all the things you should not do.

3. Complete the table below.

Caring for house plants

Things you should do	Things you should not do

Name _____

Fact and fiction

❏ Below is a list of points about cars.
Some of the points are TRUE – they are FACTS.
Some of the points are MADE UP – they are FICTION.

❏ Beside each point write FACT or FICTION.

Most cars have four wheels.

Someone who mends cars is called a dentist.

Cars run on fossil fuel.

You can put luggage in a car's engine.

Cars need Coca Cola in their engines.

Unleaded petrol is better for the environment than leaded petrol.

You are allowed to take your driving test when you are nine years old.

Some cars can fly.

Someone who mends cars is called a mechanic.

Fast car racing is sometimes called Formula 1.

You can put suitcases in a car's boot.

❏ Think about your school and write down three facts about it.

1
2
3

❏ Now write three made-up things about your school.

1
2
3

Name _____

Sasha's journey

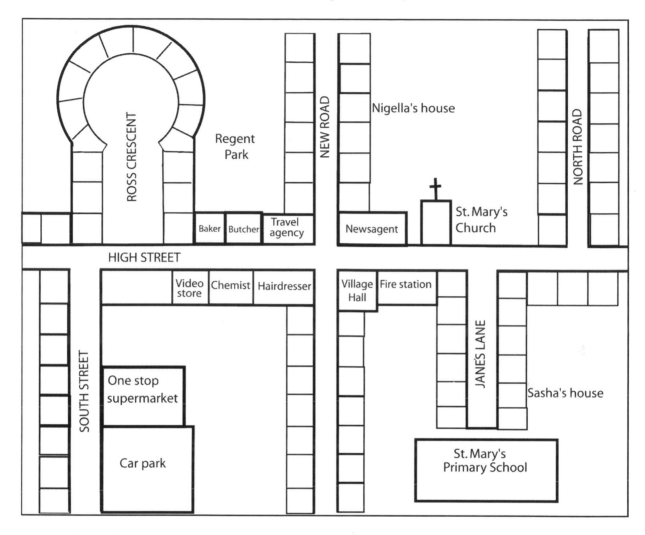

❑ Complete this text using the map above.

Sasha left the 'One Stop Supermarket' and walked up _____ Street to the _____ Street. She turned _____ to walk to the video store to return a video. She then went next door to the _____ to collect a prescription. Over the road she could see her friend Nigella standing outside the _____. She called out to her. Nigella waited while Sasha crossed the _____ Street and together they turned _____ into _____ Road where Nigella lived. After having a cup of tea, Sasha said goodbye to Nigella and walked to the newsagent. She then crossed the _____ Street again, turning _____ into _____ _____ to go home.

Name _____

Football magazine

❏ Below is the contents page from a new football magazine called Football First.

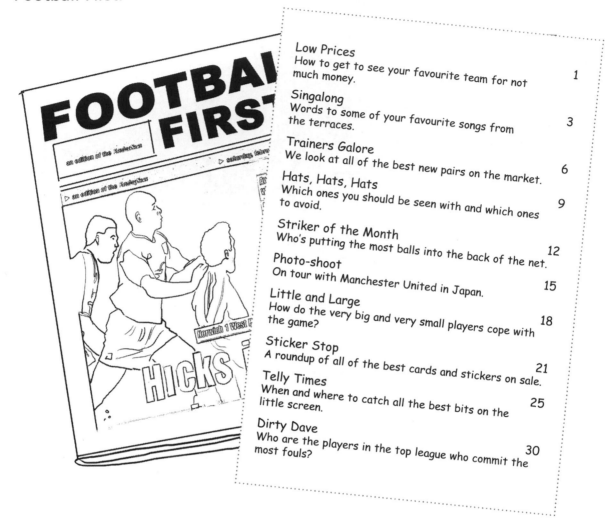

Low Prices
How to get to see your favourite team for not much money. 1

Singalong
Words to some of your favourite songs from the terraces. 3

Trainers Galore
We look at all of the best new pairs on the market. 6

Hats, Hats, Hats
Which ones you should be seen with and which ones to avoid. 9

Striker of the Month
Who's putting the most balls into the back of the net. 12

Photo-shoot
On tour with Manchester United in Japan. 15

Little and Large
How do the very big and very small players cope with the game? 18

Sticker Stop
A roundup of all of the best cards and stickers on sale. 21

Telly Times
When and where to catch all the best bits on the little screen. 25

Dirty Dave
Who are the players in the top league who commit the most fouls? 30

1. On what page of Football First and under what article title would you find information about:

   Players who score lots of goals…
   Finding football programmes on TV…
   Players of different sizes…
   A team visiting another country…
   The coolest head gear…
   Cheap tickets for football matches…

2. Now think of three other articles that could appear in Football First. Like the articles listed above, give each one a page number, title and a short sentence describing what it's about.

   _____

   _____

   _____

Name _____

Getting around

Miss Riaz did a survey. She asked the children in her class which of the following travelling equipment each of them owned: bike; roller blades; skateboard; scooter; roller skates. She found out that:

- Anna, Mike, Paul and Gina owned a bike.
- Shiko, David, Ian, Tasmin and Raya owned roller blades.
- Nick, Fatima, Alice, Ben, Steven, Zara, Yolanda and Fay owned a skateboard.
- Tina and Sam owned a scooter.
- Lara, Kevin, Lateasha and Brian owned roller skates.

She also discovered that:

- Gail owned a bike and roller skates.
- Bella and Carl owned a bike and a scooter.
- Jenny owned roller blades, roller skates and a skateboard.
- Dan, Tim, and Yurika owned none of these.

1. Use this information to plot out the graph below.

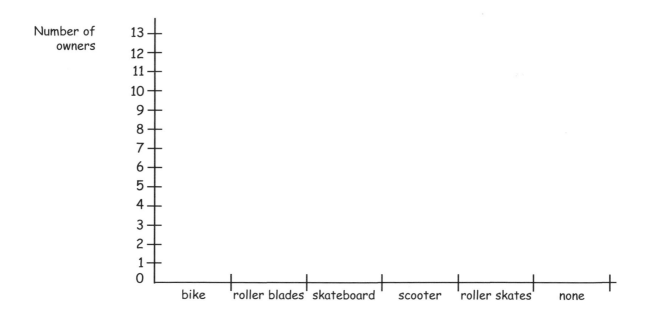

2. Which type of equipment is owned by the most children?

3. Which type of equipment is owned by the least children?

4. Give two reasons why you think skateboards are so popular with the children in Miss Riaz's class.

5. Why do you think that graphs are a good way of presenting information?

Name _____

A Roman legionary

❑ Label the picture using the information below.

A legionary wore a coat of mail for armour. He wore this over his short sleeved woollen tunic which almost reached his knees. He wore nail-studded sandals on his feet. His helmet had cheek pieces to protect his face. He protected his body with an oval shield. The legionary carried three weapons: a pilum (a long javelin); a sword which was always on his right hand side and a short dagger on his left. He carried all his belongings on a carrying pole called a furca.

Name _____

Film facts

❑ Read the following magazine article about the film industry.

Hollywood is the centre of the American film industry. Several big film companies have huge studios there, where films are made. A film is likely to be a big success if it is directed by a famous director – like Steven Spielberg. In the past ten years, children's films have started to make more and more money. This has been led by two companies – Pixar and Disney. They have worked together on many films, including Toy Story, Monsters Inc and Finding Nemo. Sometimes films are made in six months but other films can take years to make. Many films today have very good music soundtracks and in some cases these can even be as important as the films themselves. Disney have used the singer, Phil Collins, in many of their films. The cheapest films are made for under a million dollars. The most expensive ones can cost up to fifty million dollars or more.

❑ Write down the answers to these questions.

1. Where is the centre of the film industry in America?

2. Which famous director is mentioned in the article?

3. What are the names of the two companies that have worked together?

4. Name the three children's films mentioned in the article.

5. Which singer has Disney used a lot?

6. How much does a really expensive Hollywood film cost to make?

7. Write down two other facts about the film industry that are mentioned in this article.

Name _____

Houdini the Great

❑ The key words in a piece of text are the ones that are the most important. Here is a list of key words that appear in the passage below.

magician   Houdini   coins   cards   Hungary

magic shows   tricks   crowds   performer   America

❑ Underline the key words in the passage.

Harry Houdini was born in Hungary but moved with his family to America when he was four. From a young age he was fascinated with anything to do with magic. He started off by doing small card tricks for his parents. When he was 12 he ran away from home and travelled all over America performing magic shows wherever he could. As he got older he became a better performer and started to use coins in his show. Crowds of people came to watch him and he soon earned a good name as a great magician. However, after a while he got tired of using cards and coins and came up with something far more spectacular.

❑ Use the key words from the passage to help you answer these questions.

1. What interested the young Houdini?

2. What did he do on his journey round his country?

3. After cards what new thing did he introduce into his act?

❑ Here is some more information about Harry Houdini. Underline the words that you think are the key words in this passage.

Houdini started to perform acts of escape. He asked people to tie him up in ropes and handcuffs and he would then get out of these. His shows became more daring and in one act he was locked inside a tank of water and had to get out. In another display he was tied up and placed inside a locked wooden box. The wooden box was then thrown into a river! Houdini managed to untie himself and get out of the box. The spectators watching on the riverbank thought he was amazing. Away from magic, Houdini was very interested in planes and he performed a record flight in a bi-plane in Australia in 1910.

Name _____

Smoke alarm

❑ Read the following passage carefully. It is a firefighter's report about a blaze at a Town Hall. When you have finished reading it, list what you think are the FIVE main points from the report.

We were called to the Town Hall at 8.30pm. A Mrs Townsend called 999 to say she could see smoke rising from one of the upper floor windows. We were on the road in under a minute and reached the building in four minutes. When we got there, lots of smoke was billowing from the top floor of the building and it was clear that the fire was centred up there. That meant that Tony and I had to go up on the ladder as quickly as we could to get to the centre of the fire. When we reached the roof, I smashed two of the windows with my hammer and we quickly got inside. It was very dark and smoky in there but it soon became clear to us that the fire was coming from the far side of the room. We made it over there and, using our fire extinguishers, it took us approximately three minutes to put the fire out. The fire had been started in a waste paper basket by someone who had dropped a cigarette inside without putting it out. Idiot! How could anyone be so stupid? Some people just don't use their brains. If we hadn't got there so soon the whole place could have burned down and people could have died.

FIVE MAIN POINTS FROM THE REPORT:

1.

2.

3.

4.

5.

1. How do you think the firefighter felt about the person who started the fire?

2. What words or phrases make you think this?

3. What do you think will happen to the person who dropped the cigarette in the waste paper basket?

Name _____

Museum mess

❑ List as many points as you can that describe what is wrong with this class's behaviour at the local art gallery.

❑ On another sheet of paper write the answers to these questions.

1. What three key phrases could you use to describe this class's behaviour at the museum?

2. What three things might their teacher say to them when they get back to school?

3. Do you think their teacher will take them on another school visit? Why/why not?

Name _____

Park raid

The park was empty and completely dark.
The wind blew an icy chill through the air.
White snow patches settled on trees and bushes.

The driver of the van slowly backed it towards the tennis courts. The man beside him in the passenger seat gave him a thumbs-up sign. They got out of the van and met another three men who were waiting for them outside. The driver opened the back of the van. The men picked up a sack each from the ground and started loading something from the back of the van into the sacks. It was money – thousands and thousands of pounds.

"We were lucky when we made the grab," whispered one of the men to the others. "There were only two customers in there and they were both old ladies. No trouble at all." The others laughed and carried on stuffing the bank notes into their sacks.

Suddenly there was an enormous noise as about 30 armed police officers sprang out of the bushes, shouting at the men. The noise of a police helicopter whirred overhead, its beam shining on the men. The men could do nothing. They were completely surrounded. Four of the men were put in handcuffs, but the police left the driver alone.

One of the policemen walked over to the driver and patted him on the back. "You did a really good job, John," he said smiling. "I'll see you in the office tomorrow."

1. What time of day was it?
2. Describe the weather in your own words.
3. How many men were there in the park?
4. What were the men doing?
5. Where did they get the money from?
6. How did the police catch them?
7. How do you think the four other men felt about John, the driver?
8. Why do you think the first three lines of this story opening are set out as separate lines?
9. From this opening scene what do you predict might happen next in the story?

Name _____

Book search

❑ Read this story opening carefully and answer the questions after each section of text.

"That's the third time you've asked for that book this week and it's still not in," snapped Miss Dane angrily. "It's very popular at the minute and everyone's after it." She wiped the sweat from her forehead.

1. Where does this scene take place?
2. How would you describe the atmosphere at the start of this story?

Kerry shrugged her shoulders and walked away from the lending desk. Miss Dane didn't look too pleased. Kerry couldn't find The Magic of the Purple Dragon anywhere.

Kerry stood in the shade of a tree outside and suddenly a thought came to her. Her best friend, Frank, had told her about a new internet site he'd found called Kidsbooks.co.uk. He'd said that they had everything – books, dictionaries, comics. But then another thought struck her. She was banned from using the computer after she accidentally broke the new printer. Perhaps her older brother Gary would order it for her.

3. What book is Kerry looking for?
4. Where does Kerry think she might be able to get a copy of the book?

But she hadn't been very nice to him recently and he hadn't liked finding the massive spider under his pillow. It was worth a try though. If she talked about football to him that evening maybe he'd help her.

"Kerry!"

The voice sounded from inside.

5. Why might Kerry not be able to get the book?
6. Why might Gary not help Kerry?

It was Miss Dane. She looked far happier than she did a few minutes ago and she was waving a book in Kerry's direction.

"Someone just brought it back," Miss Dane exclaimed. "You can have this copy."

All thoughts of being nice to Gary disappeared from Kerry's brain as she finally laid her hands on The Magic of the Purple Dragon.

7. Why is Miss Dane looking happier?
8. Why does Kerry stop thinking about being kind to her brother?

Name _____

The story of Divali

❏ Read this story of Divali.

A long, long time ago, Prince Rama and his wife Sita were sent away from their home in Ayodhya. They were sent away by the king. Rama and Sita went far away and Rama's brother Lakshman went with them.

After walking for days and days, they found a forest and stopped there. They made a home in the forest and they made a good life for themselves. One day, something terrible happened. A ten-headed evil demon called Ravana kidnapped Sita and took her away. He took her to his island called Lanka.

Rama was very sad and worried now that Sita was gone. He knew he had to get her back, away from the evil Ravana. Rama asked the famous monkey general Hanuman to help him. Hanuman was very clever. Together, Rama and Hanuman rescued Sita. In the battle to save her, Rama killed the evil Ravana.

They had been away for fourteen years, so Rama and Sita agreed to go home. As they came back from the forest, the people of Ayodhya lit the way with special lamps called divas. As soon as Rama got home, he was crowned as the king.

The lighting of the divas has given the festival its name – Divali.

❏ Draw a cartoon strip to tell the story of Divali.

Name _____

It all ends here

❏ This is the last picture from a book called Karen Saves the Day. It is about a young girl who takes on an entire fleet of alien invaders who wish to destroy Earth. Karen wins the battle and saves the planet.

1. What do you think Karen is saying as the alien space ship flies away?

2. What could some of the people coming out of their houses be saying to Karen?

3. What words could you use to describe Karen's personality?

4. Write the ending of the story as you think it would be in the book. Use the picture to help you.

Name _____

Cartoon strip

❑ Write a caption below each of these six cartoon pictures.

1. Draw the next three cartoon pictures for this sequence.

2. Write captions to go with them.

3. Write six bullet points outlining what happens in this cartoon.

Name _____

The dragon returns

❏ This is an outline of the beginning of a film called The Dragon Returns.

A dragon is seen lurking at the bottom of a valley below a town. The people ask the bravest knight to go into the valley to fight the dragon. The dragon breathes fire at the knight and the knight runs away. The knight tells everyone in the town about how terrifying the dragon is. A small girl steps forward and says she wants to go and see the dragon. The girl starts to walk down the valley towards the dragon.

❏ What are the six key things that happen in this beginning? Draw them into the storyboard below. Describe what is happening in each scene.

Name _____

The evil wizard

❑ Here is a description of the main character from a story called
The Evil Wizard by Gail Robbins.

The wizard wore a long pointed black hat. His eyes were a sparkling green
colour and his teeth were very crooked. He had a long white beard with a
knot at the bottom.

He wore a long black cloak with numbers written all over it and long
slippers that curled up at the toes. He carried a slightly bent magic wand
in one hand and an old suitcase in the other.

❑ From the information above, design a poster advertising this book,
showing what the wizard looks like. Don't forget to put the title and
the author's name on your poster.

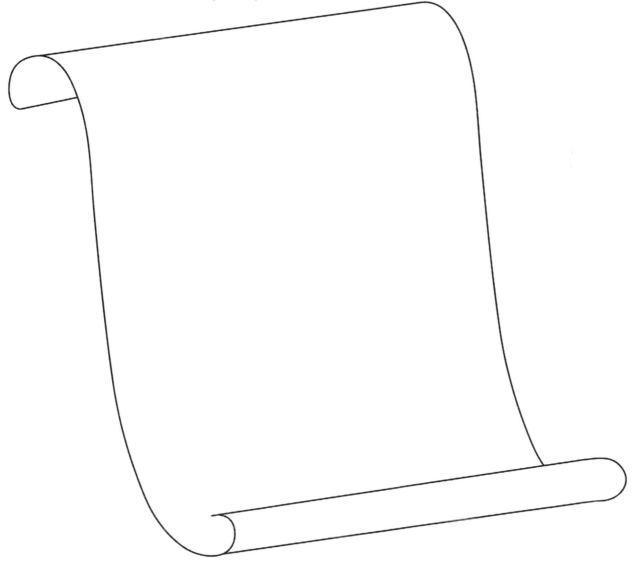

Name _____

Treasure map

❑ This is a pirate's treasure map giving instructions on exactly where a huge chest of gold and silver lies buried on an island. By studying the map carefully, answer the questions below.

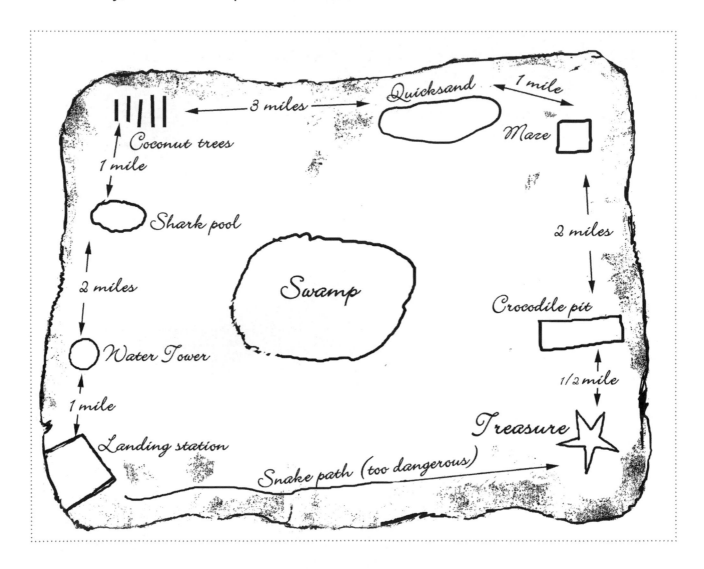

1. Why is the middle part of the map a dangerous area?

2. Name two other areas of danger on the map.

3. How far is the total journey from the landing station to the treasure?

4. Where would you go if you needed a drink?

5. Where would you go if you needed some food?

6. What is the final obstacle before reaching the treasure?

Name _____

The new girl

❑ Jenny has had a bad day in school. A new girl called Sandra has joined her class and has spent the whole day being horrible to Jenny. Here is Jenny's diary entry for this day.

A new girl joined our class today. She sat next to me and started calling me names as soon as she'd sat down. She copied my answers in the spelling test and nicked my rubber. At playtime she tried to join in our football game but kept on pushing me over. At lunchtime she stole my chocolate biscuit and threw my lunchbox on the floor. All through the afternoon she kept on pinching me until Miss Ford saw this and told her to stop. At the end of the day she said 'See you tomorrow' with a horrible look on her face.

❑ Imagine you are Jenny. Write a letter to your best friend, Anna, who lives in Australia. In the letter write a character portrait of Sandra in your own words, using the information from Jenny's diary entry above. Don't forget to put your address in the top right-hand corner of the letter.

Name _____

The Good Samaritan

❑ Complete the poem below.

Who is My Neighbour?
By David Harmer

From Jerusalem to Jericho
the road was lonely, narrow, slow.

A man came walking down the track
as thieves crept up behind his
_____.

They knocked him down and beat his head
stripped him, robbed him, left him for
_____.

He lay there bleeding in the dirt
moaning, groaning, badly
_____.

The sun burned down, his throat ran dry
but then a priest came passing
_____.

'Water please,' cried out the man.
'Priest, help me any way you
_____.'

No help came, he was denied
the priest walked by on the other
_____.

A second priest ignored his plight
just walked away and out of
_____.

As a Samaritan drew near
he shouted out in pain and _____.

'My wife and children will grieve for me
I am in the hands of my
_____.'

But with those hands his wounds were bathed
they raised him up and he was
_____.

Carried as a donkey's load
to an inn along the _____.

Washed and bandaged, laid to sleep
two silver coins left for his _____.

'Take care of him,' said his new friend
'I'll pay whatever else you
_____.'

'And when he wakes let him know
I was his neighbour not his
_____.'

1. Where was the man travelling to?
2. Were there many other travellers on the road?
3. What did the thieves actually do?
4. What did the first priest do?
5. What did the second priest do?
6. Who rescued him?
7. Where did they take him? On what?
8. What did they do to help?

Name _____

Class jobs rota

❑ Miss Bennett has a timetable pinned to her notice board. It tells her children what jobs they are doing on which day of the week.

	MONDAY	TUESDAY	WEDNESDAY	THURSDAY	FRIDAY
Milk collection	Anne	Ben	Ahmed	Sabrina	Jez
Pencil sharpening	Paul	Gill	Keesha	Jez	Iman
Reading folders	Harry	Tyrone	Carol	Grant	Ben
Tidy library	Jez	Alice	Anne	Keesha	Bill
Give out letters	Tyrone	Sabrina	Jez	Grant	Bill
Recycling bin	Keesha	Carol	Ben	Harry	Gill

❑ Write the answers to these questions on another sheet of paper.

1. Which child has the most jobs in the class? Name all of the jobs.

2. Which child or children have the least jobs? Name them and their jobs.

3. How many children have two jobs during the week? Name all of them here.

4. Who's in charge of tidying library books on Wednesdays?

5. Who is responsible for a certain type of drink on Mondays?

6. Who makes sure pencils are sharp on Tuesdays?

7. How many jobs in total are there over the course of a whole week?

8. Why do you think some children have more jobs than others?

Name _____

Bus timetable

❑ Here is a timetable for the buses in an area called Heaton.
The timetable lists the bus numbers, where they each stop
and how often they arrive.

		Starting at 6.45am then:
24 –	Heaton Place, Jesmond Park, Jart Road, Kerry Street, High Road, Railway Station	every 12 minutes
55 –	Heaton Place, Wigmore Street, Church Road, Town Hall, Community Centre, Supermarket	every 16 minutes
72 –	Jesmond Park, Davon Street, Hilltop Park, South Side, Highview Road, Long Street, Bus Terminal	every 9 minutes
78 –	Hilltop Park, Keer Bridge, Small Street, High Road, London Road, Railway Station	every 13 minutes
94 –	Supermarket, Underhill Road, Gateway Shops, Keer Bridge, Jent Street, Kopa Park	every 12 minutes
107 –	South Side, Kurner Street, Place Nursery, Crescent Road, Garth Road, Brent Shopping Arcade	every 20 minutes

1. Which is the least regular bus?

2. Which is the most frequent bus?

3. Which bus would you take if you wanted to go to Kopa Park?

4. What bus has Keer Bridge as its second stop?

5. Which two buses go to South Side?

6. What is the fifth stop on the number 55 route?

7. If you needed to catch a train which two buses could you take?

8. Which bus would you take if you wanted to end up at a place where there were lots of stores?

Name _____

The day trip

❑ Mr Sett's class are going on a river outing next week to look at creatures that live in rivers. These are Mr Sett's instructions about what they will be doing on the day.

"We'll be taking a train out to the country and walking down muddy roads to get to the river. The weather forecast is for a windy day so be sure to wrap up warm. Remember you lose 80 per cent of your body heat through your head. The river itself is not very deep and we will be able to walk quite a way into it. Proper footwear is a must. I don't want anyone complaining about wet shoes. Trainers are out of the question. For the pond dipping, it's important that you bring your own nets – the ones we made in DT last week. It's also vital to bring those extra bits of netting, because they can rip quite easily. There are lots of animals and birds living by the river bank, such as swans and geese and if we're not too noisy there should be quite a few of them to see. We won't be coming back to school for lunch, so please bring a packed lunch. We'll be eating at some picnic tables in a field beside the river. There are also some excellent blackberry bushes and we should be able to pick quite a few to add to our lunchtime provisions. There is a small river museum and shop that we'll be visiting at the end of the day, so if you want you can bring a small amount of money, but no more than two pounds – otherwise I'll never get you out of there. Also, it's a pretty long train journey, so if you get bored easily I suggest you bring something to read."

1. From Mr Sett's instructions, make a bullet point list of everything the children in his class will need to take on the river outing. There are at least seven items but there are many others you could also recommend.

2. From Mr Sett's instructions draw a diagram of the scene of the class at the river. Include as many details as possible.

3. Do you think Mr Sett has missed anything out from his instructions? If so, what is it?

Name _____

Walking brothers

❏ Two brothers Henry and Stan are about to set off on a walk.
Henry is dressed in proper walking clothes. Stan is not.
Here is a description of what they are wearing:

Henry	Stan
Walking boots	Slippers
Waterproof coat	Dressing gown
Waterproof trousers	Shorts
Woolly hat	Baseball cap

❏ Here is a description of what they are holding:

Henry	Stan
Map	Art magazine
Water bottle	Crisps
Mobile phone	Toy rocket

❏ Draw and label a diagram of Henry and a diagram of Stan, showing
exactly what they are wearing and holding.

Name _____

The playground

❑ Look at this plan view of a playground.

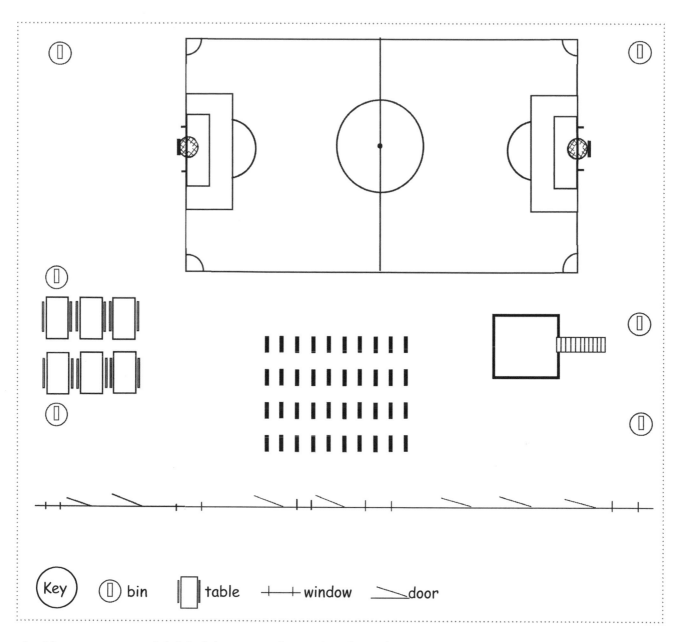

Key ⬭ bin   ▯ table   ┼─┼ window   ╲ door

1. How many rubbish bins are there in the playground?

2. How many rungs are there on the climbing frame ladder?

3. How many classrooms directly open out onto the playground?

4. What do you think the tables are for?

5. What do you think the 40 lines on the ground are for?

6. What sports do you think can be played on the games court?

Name _____

The boots

❑ Putting on a pair of football boots may seem like a very simple thing to do but there are in fact lots of steps to take if you are to do it properly. Below is a set of instructions but they are written out in the wrong order.

Have a run around to make sure they're comfortable.

Pull on your football socks over your shinpads.

Tie the laces up tight on the boots.

Put one foot into each boot.

Get the boots from your kit bag.

Put your shinpads on.

Make sure the studs are screwed in properly.

1. Write the instructions below in the right order.

　　1.

　　2.

　　3.

　　4.

　　5.

　　6.

　　7.

2. Now write four instructions for cleaning a pair of football boots.

　　1.

　　2.

　　3.

　　4.

Name _____

Fire drill

❑ Here is a list of instructions for a school fire drill. They are not written in the correct order.

Don't pick up any belongings.
Make sure all class doors are shut.
When it is clear that the building is safe, everyone may return to their classes.
Line up in classes in the playground.
Walk to the playground.
Don't shout or make a fuss on your way out of the class.
The school administrator will bring all of the class registers out into the playground.
As soon as you hear the alarm, leave the room immediately.
In the playground it is very important for everyone to be quiet and calm.
The first thing you will hear is the school fire alarm.
Your teacher will call the class register to make sure everyone is there.

1. Write these instructions as a series of numbered points in the correct order for a school fire drill.

    The first one has been done for you.

• 1) The first thing you will hear is the school fire alarm.
•
•
•
•
•
•
•
•
•
•

2. Why do you think it's so important that there are numbered instructions for a school fire drill?

Name _____

Line up

❑ Read and follow the instructions below.

1. Draw a line from left to right on this page 10 centimetres in length.
2. Write your first and last name across this line.
3. 3 centimetres below the line draw a 5 centimetre by 5 centimetre square.
4. Inside the square draw a picture of your face.
5. Underneath the square draw arrows pointing downwards to the names of all those people closest to you in your family.
6. Draw a circle around everything you have drawn and written.
7. Colour over the arrows in blue pen or ink.
8. Shade in any spaces in yellow or brown pen or ink.
9. Below the very bottom of the circle sign your name with your first initial and your last name.
10. Write the date in the bottom right hand corner of the page.
11. Now share your work with a friend. Have you both carried out the instructions correctly?

Name _____

Radio tune

❏ From looking at the diagram below, write out in order (and in your own words) the six steps you must take to select your favourite station on this car radio and at the volume you want. Can you think of any other control buttons that could be added to this car radio? Draw and label them.

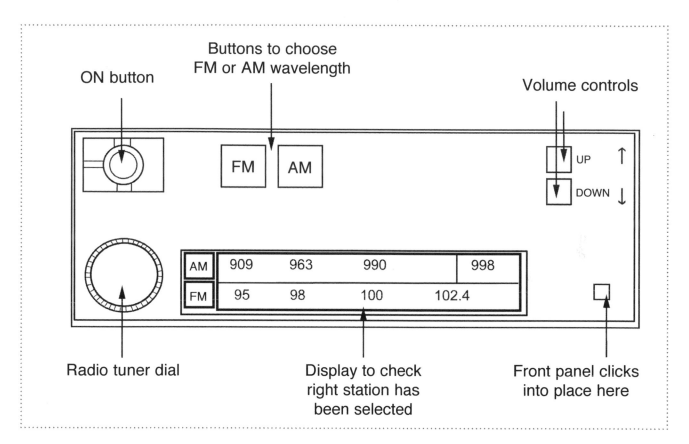

1.

2.

3.

4.

5.

6.

Name _____

Exclamation station

❑ Match the exclamations with the situations. Write each exclamation in the box below the picture.

Just because you're on two wheels!

The bins are for that!

Oi you lot – get off the grass!

Are you mad! Those things can kill you!

❑ Make up an exclamation and draw a picture for each of these situations.

Dog pulling washing off a line

Car driving into someone's front wall

Person dropping a bowl of food onto someone's carpet

Man picking apples from a farmer's orchard

Name _____

Ghost alert

❑ The six pictures below tell a story in sequence. Retell this story by writing two sentences beside each picture to describe exactly what's going on.

_____

_____

_____

_____

_____

_____

_____

_____

_____

_____

_____

_____

Name _____

The protest

There were about 30 children and adults outside the town hall. Most of them held banners and posters as they marched in a circle, stirring up all the red and yellow leaves as they walked. They held banners with messages like, 'KEEP OUR PARK OPEN!' and 'DON'T CLOSE OUR GREEN SPACE!' There was a television crew from a local station and they asked to interview Danny Holt. Danny was at the protest with his mum. The TV reporter was speaking into a phone, "Yes, I've got a kid lined up, you know, local reaction, that sort of thing."

The television reporter asked Danny lots of questions. His research on the internet and in the local library proved to be very useful. The reporter seemed impressed. When Danny finished the interview the television reporter checked her watch and hurried away. Danny heard her saying to a sound woman, "Let's see if we can make the six o'clock bulletin."

Just then a big black car pulled up in front of the town hall and a man in a grey suit got out. Someone shouted, "That's him! Mr Jones!"

Some of the people in the crowd started booing and hissing at him. Mr Jones held up his hands. Some people stopped shouting but a few continued. Mr Jones talked over the noise.

"I understand why you're all here," he said loudly, "but you can go home now because you have managed to get your way. My ring road proposal has been turned down by a planning meeting of the full council. The park will stay."

Everyone in the crowd started to cheer. Danny looked at his watch. "Better get home in time for the news," he smiled at his mum.

1. What were the people outside the town hall protesting about?
2. What time of year was it?
3. Why did the TV people want to speak to Danny Holt?
4. How did Danny know so much about the subject?
5. Why was the television reporter in such a hurry when she finished interviewing Danny?
6. Why did the crowd boo Mr Jones?
7. Why did Mr Jones hold up his hands?
8. What had Mr Jones been hoping for?

Name _____

Atmosphere

1. Write five words that describe the atmosphere in this scene.

2. What could the first sentence of this book be?

3. Think of three different titles that this book could have.

4. Make up the name of a character who lives in the castle.

5. Write a paragraph describing what you think might happen in this story.

6. If you were the artist what things would you add to the picture to make it even spookier?

7. Do you think that the first picture in a book is important? Why?

Name _____

Riddle me

❏ Read the riddles below. Work out what each riddle is about.
   Draw each item next to its riddle.

I've a dial on my front
And numbers too
Turn my dial
Get the show for you

I change my shape
In the depths of night
And though it's dark
I'm always bright

I've a hole in the middle
In a slot I go
Words and pictures
I can show

I've two small hands
And today's real date
Look at me
And don't be late

In the sports cupboard
I'm round and sit still
But when I'm kicked
Watch me speed down the hill

I'm over a hundred
And stretch up high
I sway in the wind
Below the sky

Name _____

Ricky and Dave

❑ Read the beginning of this story about two pupils at Thornton School. Ricky Smith is the class bully and is always pushing people about. No one likes him. Dave Richards is friendly with most people in the class but like everyone else tries to steer clear of Ricky.

It was Monday morning at Thornton School and Mr Thomas was late for class. Dave Richards was sitting next to Zaynab and chatting about the bike show they'd been to see on Saturday. Just then, Ricky Smith strolled into the class looking everyone up and down with a sneer. He walked over to where Dave and Zaynab were sitting and without a word of warning pushed Dave off the table. Dave fell straight onto the floor and banged his arm on the side of the table.

"What did you do that for?" shouted Dave, pulling himself up off the floor.

"That's my place," hissed Ricky. "I wanted to sit next to Zaynab, so I was just making space for myself."

"No one's got a place in this class," replied Dave.

"Don't answer me back, Richards," Ricky said as he turned his back on Dave. Dave thought about saying something else but the door opened and Mr Thomas walked into the class and started to call the register.

1. In the scene above what sort of feelings do you think Ricky and Dave are experiencing? Choose some feeling words from the list and join them with a line to the boys' names.

Ricky

angry
hurt
upset
frightened
worried
jealous

Dave

2. Think of other words that might describe how they felt. Write these new 'feelings' words under their names.

3. Think about how Ricky and Dave behaved in the scene. Write down two things that each of them did.

Name _____

Jim's model

Jim stood at the front of the class and held up his model car as Mr Sunil had asked him to. As soon as he held it up one of the front wheels fell off. The whole class burst out laughing.

"Stop that at once!" demanded Mr Sunil.

1. How do you think Jim felt when the class started laughing?
2. Why did Mr Sunil get so angry with the class?

"It's actually the best model that anyone in this class has made," Mr Sunil said. "Just because one wheel falls off it doesn't mean anything." Jim's cheeks had gone very red as he stood there. Suddenly Jim threw the model on the floor and ran out of the door. The model smashed into lots of different pieces.

3. How do you know that Jim felt embarrassed?
4. Why does Jim act as he does?

Mr Sunil followed him and found him in the corridor trying not to cry.

"It's alright," said Mr Sunil. "You know how mean they can all be. I meant what I said in there. Yours is the best."

"Seriously?" asked Jim suddenly looking a lot brighter.

He walked back into the class with Mr Sunil. His classmates looked ashamed and upset. They realised that what they'd done had been cruel.

5. What cheers Jim up?
6. Which two words show you that other children in the class are upset by their own behaviour?

Lorna Kennedy had picked up his model pieces from the floor and was trying to put them back together.

"It's OK," said Jim. "I'm sure I would have laughed if it had happened to someone else."

"Maybe," replied Lorna. "But it was a brilliant model."

"Well I'll just have to start on a new one," Jim answered, thinking about what Mr Sunil had said and already planning what his new model would look like.

7. Why is Lorna trying to put the model back together?
8. How do you think Jim feels at the end of this passage?

Name _____

Mrs Turner is angry

"Well, where is it?" demanded Mrs Turner. "Everyone else has given theirs in."

Mike shifted uncomfortably in his seat. Should he say the dog ate it? How about he dropped it down a manhole on his way to school?

No, she'd never believe him. Mike could feel 29 pairs of eyes focused on him. He peered at the class clock. Fifteen minutes and he'd be on his way home. If only he could get Mrs Turner off his back.

Mike could hear the sound of scratching behind him - pencil on paper. It was coming from Tyrone's desk.

"Well, Mike?" snapped Mrs. Turner. "I haven't got all day. Where is it?" She started tapping her fingers on her table.

Mike was about to speak when he felt something brush against his elbow. It was a finished piece of work, written out in exactly the same style as his writing. He and Tyrone weren't the best of friends, but his mind flashed back to last summer and the day he had stood up for Tyrone in front of those Year 6 boys.

"It's here, Mrs Turner," Mike said quickly, holding up the piece of paper in the air.

His teacher walked over to his desk and snatched the piece of paper. She looked at it very carefully and tutted to herself.

She walked back to her desk and placed the piece of paper on top of the pile.

"You were lucky this time, Mike," she muttered. "Next time you might not be."

1. Why is Mrs Turner having a go at Mike?

2. What is Tyrone doing?

3. What are the other children in the class doing?

4. How would you describe how Mrs Turner was feeling?

5. Who helped Tyrone? Why?

6. Why do you think Mrs Turner tuts?

7. Why will Tyrone's work fool Mrs Turner?

Name _____

Tree house trouble

❑ This story is told in seven paragraphs, but they are in the wrong order. Cut out each of the paragraphs and put them in the CORRECT order.

The council road planning committee had a very long meeting. Mrs Sharp showed everyone the petition the children had made. At the end of the meeting it was decided that the new road would not be built. The tree house tree would be left alone.

Annie told the man there was no way he could allow the tree house tree to be chopped down. She said she and her friends would try and stop the new road being built. She ran over to Ben and Wendy's house to tell them the news.

The children collected a thousand signatures and gave the petition in to the woman in charge of road planning at the local council. Her name was Mrs Sharp and she sat down with the children and listened to their protest.

The children had a big party to celebrate their saving of the tree house. A photographer from the local newspaper came to take their photo. At the weekend there was a big photo of them in the newspaper under the headline, 'KIDS SAVE TREE HOUSE!'

At the start of the summer holiday, there was a knock on Annie's front door. Annie's mum opened it. A man was standing outside. He said that a new road was going to be built and that some of the trees in the wood needed to be chopped down. These included the tree with the tree house.

The tree house in the woods next to Annie's house was Annie, Ben and Wendy's favourite place in the world. In the summer they spent most of their time in it, having picnics, talking and reading books.

Wendy said they should make a petition. Ben said a petition was a letter signed by lots of people to protest about something. They needed to make a petition against the trees being chopped down and the new road being built.

❑ Draw and label three different pictures that show a scene from this story.

Name _____

The room

Yousuf walked to the end of the corridor and stood in front of the black door. He reached out for the handle and turned it slowly. He took three steps and was inside the room.

The room was a large rectangle. The door Yousuf had walked through was in the middle of one of the rectangle's shorter sides. Facing him was the other short side. On this opposite wall, there were two round windows and a poster showing a countryside scene. There were no other windows in the room.

On the right wall there were three beds. Each bed had a table beside it with a light on top. There was also a small bookshelf beside each of these tables. Each one of these had exactly the same books on it – ten children's adventure stories about space travel.

On the left wall there were three desks. Each desk had a computer on it. The computers were switched on and each one showed a picture of the planet Mars. In front of each desk, there was a blue computer chair and a small round table with a red phone. Beside each desk was a waste paper basket. Each basket had exactly the same amount of rubbish in – three old magazines.

The room was well lit. At each of the four corners of the ceiling was a large oval-shaped light and there were 20 tiny lights spread across the rest of the ceiling in four rows of five.

In the exact middle of the ceiling there was a square panel that looked as if it led up to some sort of loft or attic. The floor was covered in a thin grey carpet that was perfectly clean.

Yousuf looked round the room carefully. There was something about it that didn't seem real. It looked more like a film or television set. Suddenly he heard a voice somewhere in the distance and quickly stepped further into the room and closed the door behind him.

1. From the description given in this passage, draw a side view of the room described. Make sure you include every item that is mentioned.

2. What do you think the room is for?

3. Make up a title for a story that includes this passage.

Name _____

Teacher pun

Mrs Build is very handy
Mr Sun has a warm personality
Miss Cross has a terrible temper
Mr Bat flits around
Ms Tree barks at us
Miss Ears is a great listener
Mr Book is an avid reader
Mr Puzzle talks in riddles
Ms Cold is forever sneezing
Miss Pen writes concerned notes
Mr Pun plays with words
Ms Hunt is great at finding things
Miss Sprint is a great runner

❑ Invent a name for a teacher who fits each description below:

DESCRIPTION	TEACHER
Difficult to understand	
A big letter writer	
Always shouting	
So speedy	
Good for lost property	
Great to talk to	
Can't stay still	
Can be found in the library	
Very friendly	
Likes building things	
Is very funny	
Needs a huge handkerchief	
Very bad tempered	

Name _____

Park protest

❏ Mrs Mates thinks the children's equipment in her local park is not safe. She has written a letter of complaint to Mr Jones, the local councillor in charge of parks.

Dear Mr Jones

I am writing to complain most strongly about Cherry Tree Park and the children's playground. The playground has not had any work done to it for the last five years and the equipment is now old and dangerous. To give you three examples: 1. At the bottom of the slide there is a huge block of concrete. Children going down forwards on that slide could seriously hurt their heads; 2. The metal bolts that hold the swings in place are no longer safe or secure. 3. There is not enough wood chip on the floor by the high climbing frame and the floor below this is clearly not a safe surface for a child to fall upon.

It will not be long before someone has an accident. I trust that you will take these points seriously and do something about them. I am not the only person who feels angry about these matters. Many other people in the community are also very worried about the safety of the playground. In fact if something is not done soon I will get together a petition and send it to our local member of parliament and the local newspaper. I expect a response to this letter as soon as possible.

Yours sincerely
Mrs Gillian Mates

1. With which two words does Mrs Mates describe the equipment?
2. What does she think might happen soon if the equipment is not upgraded?
3. What mood was she in when she wrote the letter?
4. What does she say she will organise if things don't change?
5. What will she need for the petition?
6. Apart from her member of parliament and the local newspaper, who could she contact?

Name _____

Sport girl

❏ Polly Smith is interested in joining a sports club and she writes a letter of enquiry to the manager of the club.

> Polly Smith
> 11 Beech Drive
> Baytown

The Manager
Splash Sports Club
22 Learner Road
Baytown

Dear Sir

I am very interested in joining your club, but there are some things I need to know before I join. I'm interested in the swimming pool but I don't know how long it is or how deep the deep end is. Could you let me know please? I'd also be interested in trying out one of the athletics classes but don't know if it's for people my age or what day it's on. I'd also like to start playing tennis and I'm not sure if I need my own racket to play. A friend has told me that it only costs £10 to join for the year and I wanted to see if that was true. My friend also said I need to fill out a form to join but I don't know where to pick them up. I would be very grateful if you could answer these questions.

Yours faithfully
Polly Smith

❏ Polly asks seven questions in her letter of enquiry. Write each one of them out with a question mark.

1.

2.

3.

4.

5.

6.

7.

Name _____

Phone book scan

❑ This is a page in a telephone directory. Study the entries and then answer the questions below.

ALBERT Arthur
27 Primrose Drive   09899 0982777

ALBERT Dr John
56 Turner Avenue   0784637 09883

ALBERT Mrs R
44 Howard Road   09873 672773

ALBION Simon
78 Young Street   08763 738373

ALBION T
67 Randall Road (home and vet practice)   0986346 92728298

ALISSON Deirdre
112 Town Close   083663 872373

AMERTON Peter & Jane
344 Underwood Grange   0837363 736367

1. At what address and on what phone number would you find a doctor?

2. Who lives on Turner Avenue?

3. What number would you ring if you needed someone to look after your ill dog?

4. Who would you be speaking to on an 08763 number?

5. Why do you think some people only give their first initial instead of their whole name?

6. Where would you find the house of the female ALBERT listed in the directory?

Name _____

Tudors and Stuarts

❑ This is an index from a history book about the Tudors and Stuarts.

Castles	....	27, 28
Clothing	....	22
Country life	....	16
Food and drink	....	29
Housing	....	19, 20
Population	....	15
The poor,	Tudors............	18
	Stuarts	23, 24
The rich,	Tudors............	17
	Stuarts	22
Wars,	Tudors............	30, 31
	Stuarts	32, 33

1. Use this index to write down on what page of the book you might find information about the following subjects:

<u>PAGE</u>

Battles in Stuart times.................................

Tudor poverty ....

Fighting in Tudor times...............................

Eating habits in Stuart times ....

The poor people of Stuart times................

Where people lived in Tudor times............

Stuart buildings ....

2. Invent a good title for the book.

3. Draw a picture that you think could be found on page 28.

Name _____

Long jump

❑ Class 3Y have been preparing for their
annual school sports day. They have been
practising the long jump. This is a graph
showing how far in centimetres they are
able to jump.

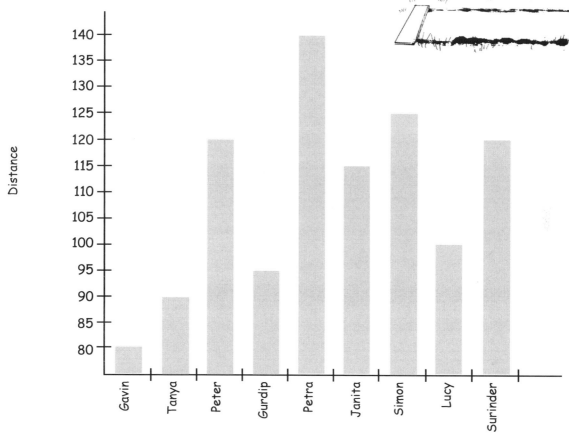

1. Who has jumped the longest distance?

2. Who has jumped the shortest distance?

3. How many children have jumped further than one metre?

4. How many children have jumped less than one metre?

5. Who has jumped five centimetres more than Tanya?

6. Who has jumped five centimetres less than Simon?

7. How do you think the long jump distances were measured?

Name _____

Heights

❑ Look at the heights of these eight children in Jamila's class.

Jamila
1 metre 10 centimetres

Dave
1 metre 15 centimetres

Karen
1 metre 12 centimetres

Ruby
1 metre 7 centimetres

George
1 metre 20 centimetres

Usman
1 metre 13 centimetres

Joe
1 metre 22 centimetres

Dinesh
1 metre 17 centimetres

1. Who is the tallest of the group?

2. Who is the shortest of the group?

3. By how many centimetres is Karen shorter than Usman?

4. Which two children are the closest in height?

5. Complete this table that states the children's heights in centimetres.

Usman   113...centimetres
Ruby   ....centimetres
Dave   ....centimetres
Dinesh   ....centimetres
Jamila   ....centimetres

Name _____

Distances

❏ Clare wants to write a directory detailing all the journey times of her classmates to school. Here is her research so far:

Everyone from our school comes from so many different places. Some kids live next door and some travel miles. I've done a survey of a few kids in my class and the differences in travelling time and distance are amazing. Samina and Kate both live five miles away but while it takes Samina 20 minutes to get to school it takes Kate an hour. Grace lives two miles away and her journey time is 20 minutes which is the same time as Alan's but he only lives half a mile away and spends ages in the sweet shop. Howard's flat is ten miles away and he has to take two buses for the hour and ten minute journey. Jain's house is a mile away but she walks with her younger sister and takes 40 minutes. Pete lives next door to Jain but he cycles, so he makes it in to school in ten minutes. I'm Clare and I live just over three miles away and I get the train and it takes me 35 minutes.

1. Complete the table below using all the information that Clare has recorded above.

Name	journey time	distance

2. Who lives the furthest from school?

3. Who lives the nearest?

4. Whose journey time is the shortest?

5. Whose is the longest?

6. Why do some children take different lengths of time to get to school even though they live the same distance away?

Name _____

The chess club

❑ Annie Dixon is her class's representative on the school council.
She wants there to be a lunch time chess club for children in the school.
This is a speech she makes to her class.

"I think there should be a lunchtime chess club because not everyone wants to play outside during the lunch break. Chess is a great game and it really makes you think hard. I know that a teacher would need to be there but I'm sure someone would be happy to do it. I think the club would have to have a maximum of 20 children otherwise it would be too big. Already some children have told me that they would be interested in joining a chess club. I'm very happy to ask the head teacher about the starting of this club but wanted to ask all of you first what you think about it."

❑ Write notes that cover all the main points Annie makes in her speech.

1.

2.

3.

4.

5.

6.

7.

Name _____

Jeff and the cat

❏ Events can be written about in many different ways. They can be headlines in newspapers, stories, letters, one paragraph summaries or diary entries.

❏ Read the short account below.

A cat got stuck in a tree in the school playground during the lunch hour. Two teachers tried to get it down but it didn't move at all. Then Jeff from Year 3 asked the teachers if he could have a go. They said OK but told him to be careful. Jeff climbed very slowly up the tree talking to the cat all the time. The cat looked at Jeff very carefully. Jeff climbed onto the branch where the cat was standing and whistled to it for a few seconds. The cat slowly walked towards Jeff and he held it in his right hand. He then climbed down the tree using his left hand and his feet. The cat was purring by now. Everyone around, even the teachers, clapped Jeff.

❏ Write about the above account in a number of different ways.

1. First write it as a HEADLINE for the school magazine.

   _____

2. Now write it as a ONE PARAGRAPH SUMMARY for the local newspaper.

   _____

   _____

   _____

   _____

   _____

3. Now write it as a DIARY ENTRY from Jeff's writing book.

   _____

   _____

   _____

   _____

   _____

Name _____

Town map

❑ Study this map and use it to answer the questions below.

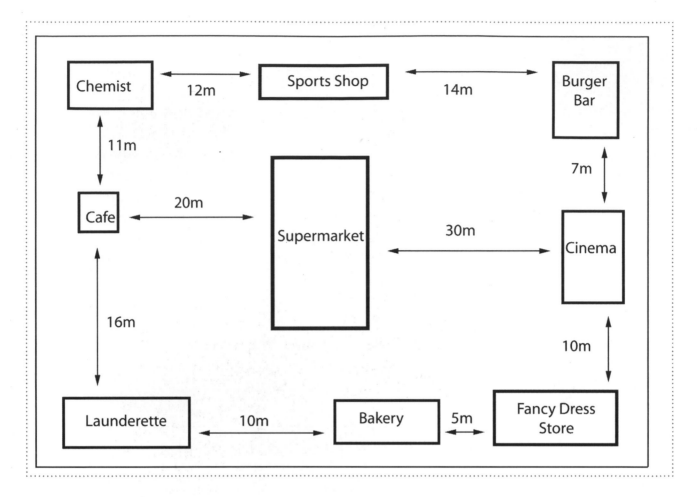

1. Where would you go to buy cough sweets?

2. How far is it from the café to the cinema?

3. Which two shops would be useful if you needed to go to a party?

4. What is the biggest distance marked on the map between two buildings?

5. How many metres would you have to walk to go from the launderette to the bakery?

6. How far is it to walk round all of the shops in a circle starting at the Burger Bar and ending at the Sports Shop? (Don't include the Supermarket.)

7. Think of two new shops that could be opened in this town.